Samuel French Acting Edition

Drop

by Dano Madden

SAMUELFRENCH.COM   SAMUELFRENCH.CO.UK

FOR PRODUCTION ENQUIRIES

UNITED STATES AND CANADA
Info@SamuelFrench.com
1-866-598-8449

UNITED KINGDOM AND EUROPE
Plays@SamuelFrench.co.uk
020-7255-4302

Each title is subject to availability from Samuel French, depending upon country of performance. Please be aware that *DROP* may not be licensed by Samuel French in your territory. Professional and amateur producers should contact the nearest Samuel French office or licensing partner to verify availability.

MUSIC USE NOTE

Licensees are solely responsible for obtaining formal written permission from copyright owners to use copyrighted music in the performance of this play and are strongly cautioned to do so. If no such permission is obtained by the licensee, then the licensee must use only original music that the licensee owns and controls. Licensees are solely responsible and liable for all music clearances and shall indemnify the copyright owners of the play(s) and their licensing agent, Samuel French, against any costs, expenses, losses and liabilities arising from the use of music by licensees. Please contact the appropriate music licensing authority in your territory for the rights to any incidental music.

IMPORTANT BILLING AND CREDIT REQUIREMENTS

If you have obtained performance rights to this title, please refer to your licensing agreement for important billing and credit requirements.

DROP was performed on April 25, 1996 at the Morrison Center Stage II in Boise, Idaho under the direction of the playwright; the lights were designed by Karena Nielsen; the original music was by Carolyn Bevington. The cast was as follows:

ORFLONG .... Samuel Read
ZIP .... Randy Davison
DROP .... Sara Bruner

DROP was performed as a Kennedy Center American College Theatre Festival entry on December 7, 1996 in Stage II of the Morrison Center in Boise, Idaho. The same production was performed at The Kennedy Center on April 22, 1997. This production was directed by Micheal Baltzell; the lights were designed by Karena Nielsen; the costumes were by Josie Jensen; the original music was by Carolyn Bevington; the stage manager was Kristy Martin. The cast was as follows:

ORFLONG .... Nick Garcia
ZIP .... Dwayne Blackaller
DROP .... Amber Hartley

DROP was further developed during the week of April 26 through May 4, 1997 at The Bonderman IUPUI National Youth Theatre Playwriting Development Workshop in Indianapolis, Indiana. The director was Peter Brosius and the dramaturg was Deborah Frockt. The cast was as follows:

ORFLONG .... Alexandra Aufderheide
ZIP .... Rob Johansen
DROP .... Diane Timmerman

PLANET DWELLERS

ORFLONG

ZIP

DROP

PLAYWRIGHT'S NOTE:

The language spoken in the play by Zip and Orflong was created as part of the Gavanuuyian world. Immediately following each line in Orflong and Zip's foreign language is an English translation of what is being said. This translation is to give the director and actors a clear understanding of what is going on in each scene.

This play is dedicated to those who have supported me in every moment: My parents, John, Katie and Eden.

(Hunting for Kalakazula. Mysterious hunting music rises. ORFLONG enters in a crouched position moving very carefully and deliberately. He is hunting for Kalakazula, a major food source on the planet Gavanuuy. His hunting weapon, in earth terminology, is a toilet plunger connected to a larger handle taken from either a broom or a mop. He walks carefully through the field of red dirt as if he is walking through a minefield. Every few steps he stops and his actions are as follows: He carefully places the plunger on the ground, blows on the handle, taps the top of the handle three times hard, and then sticks his ear to the end of the handle to listen for Kalakazula. [Incidentally, Kalakazula are large, worm-like creatures, about the size of a cat on earth. They can be eaten in a variety of different ways.] After listening and hearing nothing, ORFLONG moves on carefully, quietly and deliberately to another spot on the ground. After ORFLONG goes through this motion several times, he finally hits a spot where a Kalakazula has burrowed into the ground. At this moment, ZIP darts across the stage behind ORFLONG. ORFLONG continues with his regular hunting procedure, only this time he hears a Kalakazula. After listening carefully and repeatedly, he lines up the plunger, takes a specific grip on the handle and begins plunging for Kalakazula. He is very concentrated and determined to suck up one of the giant, worm-like creatures. As he works, ZIP enters behind him again. ZIP is carrying two of the long plunging devices. ZIP is not hunting for Kalakazula, though. He is playing, as ZIP always does. ZIP uses the plungers as giant legs of a monster. He walks as though he is a giant beast. He is very

7

slowly sneaking up on ORFLONG. ORFLONG does not notice ZIP. He is too busy plunging for what he thinks is the largest Kalakazula he has ever tried to catch. ZIP sneaks up behind ORFLONG, raises his plunger legs and makes a charge right at ORFLONG's butt. ORFLONG is knocked flying on his face, butt, etc. . .)

ORFLONG. OOOOzzaaa! Zip! Urla fluka merny!? [Ouch! Zip! What're you doing!?]

(ZIP raises his plungers to make the final kill on ORFLONG.)

ZIP. *(Monster moans)* Gruuuuuuuuuuuuuuuuuuuuuuuuu-uuu!! Acka Hugggga, Doooga, Mooola heepa! AAAAAAAA AAuuuughhhhhhhhhhhhhhhhhh!

(ZIP begins to plunge ORFLONG's belly.)

ORFLONG. Zip! Lappa Buul! [Zip! Stop it!]
ZIP. Gruuuuuuuuuuuuuuuuuuuuuuuuuuuuuuuuuuu!!!
ORFLONG. Ziiiiiiiiiiiiiiiiiiiiiiiiiiiiiiiiip!

(ZIP continues to plunge ORFLONG's belly. ORFLONG begins to laugh.)

ORFLONG. *(Giggling)* Zihihihihihihihihihihihihihip!
ZIP.GruGruGruGruGruAgaAgaMMMMMMMMMM-MMMMM!
ORFLONG. Tallahoooo! Nif nar lekka flay fluka lunt buul! [Alright! If that's the way you want it!]

(ORFLONG rolls over and grabs his Kalakazula stick. He

does a series of elaborate twists and turns and rises to his feet, holding up his stick as a weapon.)

ORFLONG. Peppipol nilla filla! Orflong doolis goonan squibble mullust! Rethel aaaooo fluka slimle eadst! [Episode 36. Orflong vs. the giant squibble monster. Come on you slimy beast!]

(They begin to slowly circle each other. ORFLONG occasionally lunges at ZIP with his stick. ZIP waves the sticks around as though they were giant extensions of his arms. They continue to fight. The battle is long, grueling and always dramatic. ORFLONG swipes at ZIP and ZIP falls to the ground. ORFLONG sits on top of ZIP's chest and stabs him with the plunger, screaming. ZIP's body flys up in a dramatic death convulsion. ORFLONG repeats this stabbing action and ZIP's body repeats it's convulsion. ORFLONG then stabs the plunger into ZIP's chest and begins to twist; ZIP writhes in pain. After a moment, ZIP falls, apparently dead. ORFLONG rises and let's out an absurdly long victory scream while running around the stage.)

ORFLONG. AAAAAuuuuuuuuuuuuuuuugggggghhhhh-hhh!!!!

(He stops & stares at ZIP. Pause.)

ORFLONG. Zip...Zip? Zip, appa fluka hunnle? [Zip, aren't you hungry?]
ZIP. GruGruGruhalaooooooooooooooo.

ORFLONG. Noly, Rethel aaaaooooo Zip. AAA hupe fa rizz goonan salpy befel fluka gaggappamala. [No, come on Zip. I had a really big one before you attacked me.]

ZIP. GruGrukaGrukaaaaaaaaaaaaaaaa?

ORFLONG. Zip?

ZIP. Orflong?

(Pause)

ORFLONG. Rethel aaaooo, palup thurz durp sumba uga zurd herkp mela calapin sumzin Kalakazula. [Come on, put those to some use and help me catch some Kalakazula.]

ZIP. Orflong? Orflong. Orflong!

ORFLONG. Zip, rethel aaooo. [Zip, come on.]

ZIP. Tallahoo Orflong, tallahoo. AAAA herkpt. [Okay Orflong, okay. I'll help.]

ORFLONG. Goola. [Good.]

(ORFLONG goes back to working the same way that he was at the beginning of the scene; carefully and methodically. ZIP begins to stalk around the hunting path with huge strides. Occasionally he makes a wild lunge at a piece of dirt with his plunger stick.)

ZIP. *(Plunging and lunging)* AaaaaaaaaaaaaAAAaaAA-Aaaaaghghghghghghgh!!!

(ORFLONG looks up from his work for a moment. ZIP continues to stalk.)

ZIP. *(Diving at the ground with his stick.)* Goooooooooo-ooga!

ORFLONG. *(Yanking his ear away from his hunting tool in pain)* Rethel aaaooo Zip! Flukard olpa nerny derp sakalzoo telm alfry. [Come on Zip. You're only going to scare them away.]

ZIP. Orflong, thurz poucha ilsa querka elepool. [Orflong, this patch is quite empty.]

ORFLONG. Buul ilsa frota! AAA hlap fa goonan derl perst fa calill selopnizz halgon! [It is not! I had a huge one just a few seconds ago!]

ZIP. AAAA yas buul fa banan poucha. Kooka woha dreza buul ilsa. Thune dirga ilsa olpa goola zund elathy durp rulla nini. *(Begins to roll in the dirt)* MMMMMMMMMM-MMMMMMMMMMMMMMMMMMMMMMMMMMMM-MMMMMMMMM......MMMMMM......MMMMMMMMM-MMMMM.......MMMMMMMMMMM...........MMMMM-MMMMMMMMMMM....MMMMMMMMMMMMMMM... [I say it's a bare patch. Look how dry it is. This dirt is only good and healthy to roll in.]

ORFLONG. Dumma Zip! Nawa flukard sakalazoo telm rofe sulrp! [Dammit Zip! Now you're scaring them for sure.]

ZIP. *(Rising up)* Oda fluka wnok urla melborp ilsa Orflong? [Do you know what the problem is Orflong?]

ORFLONG. Yelsa. AAA oda. [Yes. I do.]

(Pause)

ZIP. AAA teb fluka odla neve mofrep candip folz Kalakazula, odla fluka? [I bet you did not even perform the dance of the Kalakazula, did you?]

ORFLONG. Urla? [What?]

ZIP. Candip folz Kalakazula! [The dance of the Kalakazula!]

ORFLONG. Appa fluka belpa souires? [Are you being serious.]

ZIP. Yelsa, Orflong. Buul candip ot ogdas ot gilile sunool zund wolile sunool chiw sesanc Kalakazula durp siris durp cafrus dirga. [Yes, Orflong. It's the dance to the Gods of the high sun and the low sun which causes the Kalakazula to rise to the surface of the dirt.]

ORFLONG. Fluka wokno, Zip nehew wuzi latsy mite fluka tualla toguut Kalakazula? [You know, Zip, when was the last time you actually caught a kalakazula?]

ZIP. Onwa, nif AA Samurz ganle sunools thiw yimy larfa suckna zund srox lipix tefil yimy fleff .... [Now if I measure the angle of the suns with my hunting tool and cross six feet to my left...]

ORFLONG. AA malm olpa nonu owp revan kerpas ruuooo machystoom rishoum. Appa fluka waranle olpa chiw? Oda fluka lizeal chiw, Zip? [I am the only one who ever keeps our stomachs nourished. Are you at all aware of that? Do you realize that, Zip?]

ZIP. Hmmmmmmmmmmmm.....telas esee rehreh, noonta greedaz wotards gibig liefd. Ewll nif ginby candip rehreh, Kalakazula llirew siris cafrus! [Hmmmmmmm...let's see here, 90 degrees towards the big field. If we begin the dance here, the Kalakazula will rise to the surface!]

ORFLONG. Zip. Llelly? Zipple! [Zip. Hello? Zipper!]

ZIP. Llelly, tondot llacay ememn chiw. . .Zipple. [Hey, don't call me that ... Zipper.]

ORFLONG. Rosew. Zip. [Sorry. Zip.]

ZIP. Rethel aaoo Orflong! Telas ginby candip forba sunools sroc! [Come on Orflong! Let's begin before the suns cross!]

ORFLONG. Urla.....urla ilsa ledy? [What....what is your deal?]

ZIP. AaaaAA urla? [My what?]

ORFLONG. Fluka ledy? Aa tordot.... [Your deal? I don't....]

ZIP. Rethel Aaaooo Orflong! Sunools vomle. Rethel Aaaooo....niley puf hindlebe AAA! [Come on Orflong! The suns are moving. Come on...line up behind me!]

ORFLONG. Oooooooohhhhh.....

ZIP. RuhRuh! [Hurry!]

ORFLONG. Ooooooohhhhhhh....... .

ZIP. RuhRuh!! [Hurry!]

ORFLONG. Ooooh......urla leh! [Ooooh.....what the hell!]

(ORFLONG moves behind ZIP.)

ZIP. Taw. *(Measures sky again.)* Tellyix greedaz; reh reh fluka golb. *(Points to spot)* Gebin rehreh Orflong. [Wait. *(Measures)* 86.39 degrees; here you go. *(Points)* Begin here Orflong.]

ZIP. Wonu. Lofow AA alde. [Now. Follow my lead.

(The dance is somewhat as follows: Hop twice on one leg, twice on the other leg, hop land with both legs spread apart and grunt. ZIP throws out his arms as he does this. The dance ritual can be as quirky and elaborate as desired. ORFLONG follows as best as he can.)

ZIP. Kalakazula. Kalaaaaakazula! Kalakazula! Kalakazula! Kalakazula! Kalakazula!

ORFLONG & ZIP. Kalakazula! Kalakazula! Kalakazula! Kalakazula! Kalakazula! Kalakazula!

(They almost make a full circle when ORFLONG begins to laugh. ZIP smiles at ORFLONG. ZIP begins to laugh as well. They both continue to dance as the music rises; No longer in a circle, but all over the land. ORFLONG abruptly stops dancing and points his plungers at ZIP in a fight position. He is returning to the imaginary battle they fought earlier in the scene. Hunt music returns. ORFLONG begins to hunt ZIP, slowly.)

ORFLONG. Aaaaaauuuuuuuuuuuuuuuughhhhhhh!!!
ZIP. Orflong...Orflong...nolly...Nolly! [Orflong...Orflong ... no....Noooooo!]

(ORFLONG chases ZIP off of the stage. The hunt music crossfades with more quirky dance music ORFLONG and ZIP dance back on.)
(ORFLONG and ZIP move to center stage. They are now in their home. They are sitting on the floor. Surrounding them are giant, reddish leaves from the upside down trees of their planet. There are paintings on these leaves. ORFLONG and ZIP also have journals made of these same leaves, smaller in size, though. ORFLONG is going through a pile of various leaf-paintings.)

ORFLONG. Hmmmm .... Aa kile thurz nurne. [Hmmm....I like this one.]

(ORFLONG holds up a leaf with a huge face painted on it. Not very artistic, though)

ZIP. Chiwe nurne? [Which one?]
ORFLONG. Rehreh. [Here.]
ZIP. OOhhhhh.....nar lood. [OOoohh.....that's old.]
ORFLONG. Buul din nif oloc. [It's kind of cool.]
ZIP. Kooka tala thurz nurne. [Look at this one.]

(ZIP hands ORFLONG a colorful collage.)

ORFLONG. Hmmmmmmmmmmmm........
ZIP. Oda fluka kile buul? [Do you like it?]
ORFLONG. Nehew odla fluka aipt buul? [When did you paint it?]
ZIP.Fa pukla folz luza gao. Urla oda fluka kinthik? [A couple of days ago. What do you think?]
ORFLONG. Buul frota AA vorly. [It's not my favorite.]
ZIP. Taw. *(Flips thru his journal.)* Rerg ilsa fa........hmm-mmm.... [Wait. There is a......hmmmm....]
ORFLONG. Urla chiw? [What's that.]
ZIP. Rehreh ewell appa. Onwa, thurz sogol thiw ainptop. Tawa ainptop hitty AA dera thurz. [Here we are. Now this goes with the picture. Watch this picture while I read this.]
ORFLONG. OkaOka. [Okay.]
ZIP. AAaaaaa......Olpops. Grawnory gaple. [Whoops. Wrong page.]
ORFLONG. OkaOka Zip. [Okay Zip]
ZIP. *(Flips thru pages again.)* OkaOka......rehreh ewell appa....yelsa....uh...tula AA suzle ainptop aggle....yelsa, yelsa, thurz ilsa nurne......Uh...hmmmmm.... [Okay......here we go....yes...uh...let me see the picture again....yes, yes, this is the one......uh...hmmmmmmmm.....]
ORFLONG. OkaOka Zip!! [Okay Zip!]

ZIP. *(Reads)* Noona ticka fupa kooka pupa. AA lims ethna thumle chumin gupa. Noona ticka, leapse tonol noonle AA uz AA elley nur zupa. [Pokey Stick on the ground, look up at me. I will smile at thee with much glee. Pokey stick, oh please do not poke me and I will let yee run free.]

(Pause)

ORFLONG. Tona fluka sebez kown. [Not your best work.]

ZIP. Yeallre? [Really?]

ORFLONG. Ainptop sewl riglta. Tuba meop......aaaaa-aaa.......... [The painting was alright, but the poem....aaa-aaaaa........]

ZIP. Zish. OOo..lewl. [Shit. Oh well.]

ORFLONG. AA vovel nurne fluka wosho AA tersa. [I loved the one you showed me yesterday.]

ZIP. Llelly ciep tilst ens kown. Eyp, snaw reth emsit fluka erg ut AA? Urne olpa tenslz? [That piece still needs some work. Hey, wasn't there something you were going to read to me? One of the entries?]

ORFLONG. Yelsa. [Yeah.]

ZIP. Ewell areh buul. [Let's hear it.]

ORFLONG. *(The following is acted out by ORFLONG complete with his being chased by the Giant Kalalakazula and finally eaten by the the beast. ORFLONG flips through his journal to find the entry.)* OkaOka........mmmmmmmmmm-mmmmm.......Rehreh ewell azzle. AA snaw uut narva goonan elif unan. AA dab suja nishmish plazkun Gerfle wilth Zip. Zip elnta sidny tozin rul colpnin. AA rearp thurz ropz wolwol ummple.....iyks ega llify llap rosts reiwa locors. AA lef tib zibbiz. AA snaw ratsil teaa racsil. Rulla! Rulla! Rulla! Rulla rulla rulla!!! Lirip lirip lirip!!! Feber AA lodcle rut nur, zousath Kalakazula geban rubow toul rulla. Goonan Kalakazula! Goonan Kalakazula! Goonan Kalakazula!! Goonan Paullaa Mewda!! Nur! Nur!! AA snaw Swarped whe goonan Kalakazula gega wosley. [Okay ..... ummmmmm .... here we are. I was out near the large field today. I had just finished playing Gerfle with Zip. He went inside to total our scores and I heard this sort of low rumble...the sky began to fill with all sorts of weird colors. I felt a bit dizzy and I was starting to get scared. That's when I noticed all of the dirt from the ground flying into the air. I knew at this point that I was in trouble. Before I could turn to run, thousands of Kalakazula began to burrow out of the dirt. They were not average size, though. Giant Kalakazula!! They were as big as the entire Paullaa Meadow. No! No! I screamed and I began to run, but it was too late. I was swallowed by one of the giant beasts and digested slowly.]

ZIP. Tawha fluka kenalpa febarore fluka ogle eeps? [What are you eating before you go to sleep?]

ORFLONG. Kalakazula.

ZIP. Ercpy. [Creepy.]

ORFLONG. Ercpy. [Creepy.]

ZIP. Yelsa. [Yes.]

ORFLONG. Yelsa [Yes]

(Pause)

ZIP. Gerfle?

ORFLONG. Gerfle!

ORFLONG & ZIP. Gerfle. . . Gerfle. . . Gerfle. . Gerfle!! Gerfle!!! GEEEEERFFFLE!!!

(Quirky music rises. ZIP and ORFLONG run offstage as the scene changes. They exit. The music changes as ORFLONG returns, scoping out the hills. ZIP enters playing. He is holding a plunger to each of his feet as he moves to the music. ORFLONG attempts to get his attention.)

ORFLONG. Zip...Zip...Buul lyop raif. Lopor? [Zip ... Zip ... it's only fair. Rope?]
ZIP. *(Points offstage.)* Lopor. [Rope.]
ORFLONG. Zip. . . lopor! [Zip. . .Rope!]
ZIP. Okaoka! [Okay!]

(After a moment, ZIP enters with the rope. He is pretending like the rope is a giant snake-like creature that is attacking him. ORFLONG watches impatiently. ZIP kills the rope/snake.)

ZIP. *(Handing the rope to ORFLONG)* Lopor! [Rope!]
ORFLONG. Zip, Rethel Aaoooo! [Zip, Come on!]
ZIP. Elwe.....AA gelsh. [Well....I guess.]
ORFLONG. Rethel Aaaaoooo. [Come on.]
ZIP. OkaOka. [Okay.]
ORFLONG. Derga. AA kisha sotha marzups. Yeth satpuk kilp gulgawkawaka faffle wihle. [Good. I'm sick of those worms. They start to taste like gulgakawa after awhile.]
ZIP. Wonup rewh olda AA eedup org Gainup? [Now where do I need to go again?]
ORFLONG. Wesuth nanga lililih....verp reknun.....fluka funtle... [The Southwest range of Hills.....over there....you see...]

ZIP. Yelsa..... [Yes.]

ORFLONG. Sorc evcap lililih. Garlge garl kalp ehinke neetpa. Pillish tulfy ungf poy. *(ORFLONG demonstrates killing the pillish, swinging the rope at the ground and then stabbing with the opposite end of a plunger.)* [Cross over the hills and the large lake is behind some trees. The Pillish swim near the top at night.]

ZIP. Pillish...Pillish.......

ORFLONG. Yelpa satcte tebba sotha Kalakazula. [They taste better than those Kalakazula.]

ZIP. Lirplirp, Orflong. AA eble caban onsa. [Alright Orflong. I be back soon.]

(ZIP begins to walk dejectedly off.)

ORFLONG. Zip!

(ORFLONG crosses to ZIP. ORFLONG places his hand on his own heart and then moves the same hand to ZIP's heart. ZIP returns the gesture. ZIP exits. ORFLONG turns to exit in the other direction. Suddenly there is a large flash or beam of light. There is also a large, ominous sound. ORFLONG sees this light and he hears the strange sound. [Note: This light and sound signifies an arrival. DROP's arrival. It is important that this arrival is ambiguous. It need not be as literal as a "spaceship". The audience must clearly see through staging and light and sound that something is different. Someone has arrived. DROP has arrived.] ORFLONG begins to dart around the stage in a slight panic, sometimes looking up at the sky. DROP slowly enters.

ORFLONG sees her and backs away. They begin to slowly circle one another. After a complete circle, ORFLONG starts to back away from DROP. ORFLONG then completely turns in an attempt to escape.)

DROP. *(Pointing at herself)* Drop!

(ORFLONG stops)

DROP. *(Pointing at herself)* Drop!

(ORFLONG stares at DROP)

DROP. Drop.

(ORFLONG begins to slowly walk towards her)

DROP. Drop. *(Pause. He stares.)* Drop.

(Pause.)

ORFLONG. Deeeeerrrrrooooop. . .
DROP. *(Points at herself)* Drop!
ORFLONG. Drrrrrrrrooooooop.
DROP. Drop.

(Pause)

ORFLONG. *(Points at himself)* Orflong!

(Music rises. ORFLONG and DROP dance at different corners of the stage.)

DROP. Orflong!
ORFLONG. Drrrrrooooopp!

(ORFLONG and DROP break to opposite sides of the stage and continue to dance.)

ORFLONG. Drop!
DROP. Orflong!

(They dance. DROP dances off and ORFLONG chases after her. Music crossfades with picnic music. DROP and ORFLONG return with various items to make a little picnic.)
(The picnic. ORFLONG watches DROP as she eats. Only occasionally does he munch on some food or sip a beverage. DROP wanders around the stage. There is a pause before she speaks.)

DROP. Hmmmmmmmmmmmmmm .... mmmm-mmm! Yes! Yes ... hmmmmmmmmmmmmmmmm .... How long have you lived here Orflong? Did I pronounce that correctly? Or-F-lll-ooooong?
ORFLONG. Deeerrropp.

(Pause)

DROP. It is really strange here! Hmmmmmmm ... the colors are very ... hmmmm .... their arrangement is .... hmmmmmmmm ... how would I ..... hmmmm ..... nothing....definitely nothing like I've ever seen before ..... huh-uh!

(Pause)

DROP. Very strange .... hmmmm ... but I feel very comfortable here .... different ... but yes, I am really more comfortable than I had expected to be .... Did it take you long to adjust? I mean how long have you lived here for?

(Pause)

DROP. Yes! Oooooooooo! Look at this! If I put these two crackers together they form a little spaceship ... see, it looks like a space disc .... watch ... hmmmmmmmmm ..... let's see .... I'll put some of this goop here and ... hmmmm ...... Doooooooooooooodododoolwoooooooooop!!

(ORFLONG laughs)
(DROP joins him and laughs as well)
(DROP then continues to eat)

DROP. Yes. Hmmmmmmmm .... Very strange . . . I . . . . *(She sees something in the dirt beyond where ORFLONG is sitting.)* Wow! What was that? Look behind you Orflong! I saw a weird little creature come out of the dirt. It sort of looked at me and then it burrowed back down! What is it? Do you know? Will he hurt us? He was sort of cute. Or maybe it was a she!

(Pause)

ORFLONG. Merny nar gablan. [Do that again.]
DROP. What? I'm sorry, I said look behind you.

ORFLONG. Seefa. [Please.]

DROP. Pardon. What are you talking about?

ORFLONG. Merny gibble fluka sujle ilple. [That thing you just did.]

DROP. It was in the dirt over there.

ORFLONG. Merny gibble fluka sujle ilple. [That thing you just did.]

DROP. I suppose I don't understand what you are saying.

ORFLONG. Uhhhh...Dousna. [The sound.]

DROP. What....I......

ORFLONG. Dousna! *(Picks up her crackers)* Thiw lackpiuns! [The sound! With the crackers!]

DROP. Crackers?

ORFLONG. *(Making a little spaceship.)* Tinayan capanip dul nar...... [The little crackers and that....]

DROP. Oooo....you mean........

ORFLONG. Tinayan dousna! [The little sound!]

DROP. Really?

ORFLONG. *(Handing her the crackers)* Lenup! [Please!]

DROP. Well...hmmmmmmmmmmm. . . . .

ORFLONG. Lenup. [Please.]

DROP. All I did was ... I put the two crackers together with this jelly goop ... and ... yes ... there you are .... hmmmmmmm ...yes ... here you go.

(She hands ORFLONG the ship.)

ORFLONG. *(Stares at his hand)* Dousna. [The sound.]

DROP. What?

ORFLONG. Fluka dafem tinayan capanip yiffle. *(ORFLONG attempts to make the crackers fly.)* Duuoodooop! [You made the little crackers fly.]

DROP. OOOOO, I think I see .... hmmmmmm ......
hmmmmmmmm ..... Doooo000dododooolwoooop!

(ORFLONG laughs)

ORFLONG. Yelsa! Ungaf! [Yes! Again!]
DROP. Are you kidding?
ORFLONG.Ungaf! Lenup! Dousna! [Again! Please! The
sound!]
DROP. Dooooo000000000dododododooolwoooop!!!!!!
(ORFLONG laughs) It is kind of silly. *(ORFLONG laughs)*
Doooo0000000000000dododododoooolwoop! *(Yes, ORFLONG
is still laughing) (DROP begins laughing as well)* Doooooo-
oooooooooooooooodododododooolwoop!

*(Upon this noise by DROP, DROPs sound begins to resonate
over the speakers in the theatre. Her sound, Dooooo0000
ooooooodododododoolwoop! is heard over and over again.
At this point, the picnic music also begins to rise. Only
ORFLONG hears DROP's sound. DROP continues
laughing as ORFLONG closes his eyes and listens.
ORFLONG rises and continues to listen. DROP gathers
up the picnic items and exits the stage. ORFLONG
gradually floats off to the sound of DROP's voice.)*
*(DROP enters. She is awkwardly carrying a Kalakazula
hunting pole. She walks as though she is stalking her
prey very, very carefully. She finds a spot and begins to
attempt the same routine that ORFLONG performed in
the first scene. She works for a few moments. ZIP enters
from behind her. He carries the rope from the Pillish
hunt. ZIP also has two plungers and he is holding them*

so that one extends from each side of his head like giant horns. ZIP stops. He stares at DROP for awhile. ZIP then slowly enters and begins to circle around DROP until he enters into her sightline and she sees him.)

DROP. *(Screaming, startled.)* Hiiiiiiiiiiiiiii!!

ZIP. Ooooooooooooo.........

DROP. *(Points at herself)* I'm Drop.

ZIP. Ooooooooo. . . . . . .

DROP. *(Points at herself)* Drop!

ZIP. Ooooooooooooooo!

DROP. *(Points at herself)* Drop!

ZIP. *(Points at himself)* Zip!

DROP. Zip? Is that your name?

ZIP. Zip!

DROP. Well I like that name, Zip!

ZIP. Vahnu fluka walagny vilivil rehreh? Rorp appa fluka malif rethun disly alpent. Cubaw AA ligif nelbe bunta ... lew ... wooga! [Have you always lived here? Or are you from the other side of the planet? Because I've only been gone about....well, when I left, I, I mean...Wow!!]

DROP. *(Laughing) (Points at herself)* I'm Drop.

ZIP. Yelsa! Drop! Wuna calpa kerb infra meles rof Gerfle! Geeeeeeeeeerfle! AA neamo, thaga ilsa, rof urla yasnany! [Yeah! Drop! Now we can break into teams for Gerfle! Geeeeeeerfle! I mean, that is, if you're staying.]

DROP. I ....uhhhh....yeah....thanks.

ZIP. WoooooopWeeeeeeeeeeHeeeeeeeeee!! Hangu fluka telma Orflong? [WoooooopWeeeeeeeeeeHeeeeeeeeee! Have you met Orflong?]

DROP. Orflong? Yes! Orflong! You know Orflong?

ZIP. Oooooh. . . Rof rosca fluka hangu. Fluka kawkila. Orflong lew tupa fluka ont kawkila. Talsa oof surb. Rehreh. Telmf AA hosh fluka solboluk roprop yawnka gilg pufa thawna suckna. .suckna. . .suckna. . . [Ooooh. . .of course you have. You're working. Orflong will put you to work. That's for sure. Here. Let me show you the absolute proper way to dig up dirt with that hunting tool. . .hunting tool. . .hunting tool. . .]

DROP. This?

(Holds up tool)

ZIP. Yeeeeeeeeelsa!!! [Yeeeeeeeeees!!]

(DROP is laughing)
(ZIP now begins stalking very slowly around the stage.)
(DROP laughs)

ZIP. Siiiiiiiiiiiiiiiiiiiiilp! [Ssshhhhhhhhhhhhhhhhhhhh!]

(ZIP continues stalking)

ZIP. Aaaaaaaaaahahahahahaha!BOoooooga! Wooooooo-ooga! Woooooooga dooooo!

(DROP is laughing)

ZIP. *(He slams his plunger into the ground)* Doookaaa! Fluka gonfu ot rasca hemle lala yawna!! Thelsa ganfu guglnuza tinayoom cusas AA vanpa vela selan, tubla satpuk, callil, tubla satpuk gulgakawa. Woon vomle sastle mitme?.

Mocla Drop! Telsa candip. Candip? Candip! (*He slams his plunger into the ground. Quirky music rises.*) [Dookaa! You are going to scare them all away!! These are the ugliest little suckers I have ever seen, but they taste...actually they taste like shit. Why are we wasting our time? Come on Drop! Let's dance! Dance? Dance!]

(*DROP and ZIP break into a dance. They dance for a moment before ORFLONG runs onstage doing a little dance. He stops when he sees ZIP and DROP together. He watches them for a moment. Pause. The music stops abruptly at ORFLONG's signal.*)

ZIP. Heena Orflong! [Hi Orflong.]
ORFLONG. Vuna fluka melna Drop? (*Points to DROP*) [Have you met Drop?]
ZIP. Yelsa! [Yes!]
DROP. . . .Yes.
ORFLONG. OkaOka!!!

(*The music comes back up and they all dance together.*)
(*At the end of the dance, DROP dances off. Pause. ZIP and ORFLONG stand staring at each other. A moment passes and they exit.*)
(*DROP enters, followed closely by ORFLONG and ZIP. DROP is carrying the Pillish hunting rope.*)

DROP. (*Untangles jump-rope*) Hmmmmmmmmm .....
okay, this is really pretty simple. Hmmmmmmmmmmmm
..... I have never needed to explain this before ... Hmmmmmm
.... (*Handing an end of the rope to ORFLONG*) Take this.

(ORFLONG drops the jump-rope.)

ORFLONG. Oooooooooooooooooo.....

DROP. Hold....here, hold on tight.

ORFLONG. *(Swinging the rope hard at the ground)* Pillish!! Yelsa? [Pillish!! Yes?]

DROP. Now....hmmmmmmmm.....Zip......here you go.

ZIP. *(Shaking the rope like a snake.)* Lopor! Lopor Orflong!! [Rope! Rope Orflong!!]

DROP. *(Laughing)* What are you doing?

ZIP. Ilsa thurz nurne? [Is this right?]

DROP. Let's see. . .just stand still for a second. *(She begins to feel the ground)* Hmmmmmmm. . .this ground is a little mushy, but I guess it will have to do.

ORFLONG. *(Feeling the ground next to DROP)* Nounga ilsa reperfa nof yalping Gerfle! [The ground is perfect for playing Gerfle!]

ZIP. Gerfle! Gerfle!! Gerfle!!!

DROP. Now we spread apart.

(DROP pushes them apart.)
(ORFLONG and ZIP pull the rope tight.)

DROP. No sillies!.....we need some slack!

ZIP. Nnnnnuuooooo ssiilliez. . .Nooooo sillies! Nooooo sillies!! Nooooo sillies!!! Nooooo sillies!!!

DROP. *(Laughing)* Okay, now I stand here and you guys swing the rope.

(She helps ORFLONG begin to swing the rope.)

ORFLONG. Oda hible? *(Yanks rope up and down several times hard.)* [Do this?]

DROP. No. Hmmmmmmmmmmmm .... just a nice smooth motion.

(They start)

ZIP & ORFLONG. OOoOOOOOOooOOOOOOOo. . .

DROP. Yes! That's it. Yes! MMmmmmmmmmmmmmm-mmmmhhhhmmmmmmmmmmmmmmmmmm! Here I go!

(DROP begins jumping)

ZIP & ORFLONG. OoooOOoooOoooooooooOO!!!

ZIP. Yelsa seelies! Yelsa sillies!

ORFLONG. Wheeeeeeeeeeeeeeeeeeeeeeeeeeeeeeeeee!

ZIP. Siiilly Drop! Silly Drop! Fluka murple! Silly Drop! Oda ewll murple? *(ZIP starts jumping, throwing off the motion of the rope.)* [Silly Drop! Silly Drop! You are bouncing! Silly Drop! When do we get to bounce?]

DROP. Oooops!

ZIP. Nnooo sillies!

ORFLONG. Ooooo. . .

DROP. Okay Zip, it's your turn. Would you like to go?

ZIP. Ggoo? Zip. . .ggoo. . .go. . .go!!

(ZIP begins jumping.)

(Music rises. ZIP gets tangled up in the rope as he attempts to get ORFLONG to jump. All three dance off. The jump-rope music is overtaken by sleep music. ZIP and ORFLONG return first. They yawn and cover each others mouths simultaneously as a pre-sleep ritual.)

(ORFLONG immediately lays down after his bed is made. He puts his arms behind his head and stares at the sky. ZIP pulls out some leaves and begins to draw. DROP begins to perform some meditation exercises. She creates sounds while doing this pre-sleeping ritual. ORFLONG and ZIP begin to glance at her while she meditates. ORFLONG and ZIP attempt to watch while avoiding being caught by either DROP or each other. This entire routine lasts for a few moments. DROP ends her meditation and lays down to go to sleep. ORFLONG sits up and pulls out his journal [leaves] and begins to write. ZIP still lies in bed awake. DROP is sleeping peacefully. When ORFLONG completes what he is writing in his journal, he slowly stands up and begins to walk. ORFLONG heads towards DROP. ZIP has the same idea and rises as well. They are both away from their beds. As they both circle, their eyes meet at center stage. There is a long silence as they stand looking at one another.)

ZIP. Hey.
ORFLONG. Heena.
ZIP. Telpnef niiight ooout, ilsa it? [Beautiful night out, isn't it?]
ORFLONG. Yelsa.
ZIP. Long time....nelga wilfgas we played duglon game of Gerfle. [Been awhile since we played a good game of Gerfle.]
ORFLONG. Yelsa. *(Pause)* Gerfle.

(Pause)
(ORFLONG and ZIP stand staring at one another. ZIP smiles. ORFLONG smiles back. They both slowly turn

and exit. Music rises as DROP wakes up. She exits the stage.)

(Gerfle music. ORFLONG and ZIP enter playing Gerfle. They carry their Kalakazula poles and are slamming an odd, ball-like thing around the stage. Gerfle is never played the same way twice. It is combinations and variations of all sports on earth; Including badminton, croquet, football, soccer, volleyball, tennis, basketball, hockey, polo, pool...etc. It is always exciting and wild. ZIP slams the game "Ball" down onto the ground and performs a ritual in order to score. ORFLONG catches him and attempts to block the score by screaming at the ball.)

ZIP. Schnaster, schnaster, Gerfle master! Wooooo-hooooooooooooo!

ORFLONG. Lofre! Habitiz gunoop zilly nill AA voraf, nuzun ixill zillkewer omfro fluka reol ofron nalpelaz zum.... [Foul! That's 8 zilly in my favor, minus 6 zillkewer from your area for the penalty and....]

ZIP. Whhuut!? I hhavve noot sseen fluka ccheeat thurz mmuch inn one ggaame Orflong!

(Slight Pause)

ZIP. AA vah verne esne fluka echta thurz chuma ninin enon maglf Orflong!! [I have never seen you cheat this much in one game Orflong!]

ORFLONG. AA nodo hepeze! [I don't cheat!]

ZIP. Aaaaaaaaaugh!

(DROP enters, skipping across)

ORFLONG. Frunfru Drop! [Hello Drop!]
ZIP. Selkasu Drop! [Greetings Drop!]

(DROP exits. ORFLONG steals the game ball from ZIP and runs off the stage. ZIP exits and re-enters balancing the ball on his plunger stick. ORFLONG is making a desperate attempt to knock the ball down.)
(DROP enters jumping rope.)

ZIP. Hi Drop!
ORFLONG. Frunfru Drop! [Hello Drop!]
DROP. Hi Zip!

(DROP exits. ORFLONG and ZIP both watch her leave. ZIP places the ball center stage. He and ORFLONG press butt to butt. They hop away from the ball in opposite directions.)

ORFLONG. Noen!! [One!!]
ZIP. Unkff!! [Two!!]
ORFLONG. Poiyy!! [Three!!]

(DROP enters. She picks up the ball and stands watching. ORFLONG and ZIP turn and charge where the ball was.)

ORFLONG & ZIP. Gerfle!!!!

(They stop abruptly as they see DROP with the ball.)

ZIP. Drop, Drop, Drop!!!

ORFLONG. Hhii Drop.
DROP. Hi Orflong.
ZIP. Doo you wanna play some gerfle?
DROP. Gerfle is boring.
ZIP. B.....B......Lanupa? [Boring?]
ORFLONG. Lanupa? [Boring?]
DROP. I've got a better game!!
ZIP. Better than Gerfle?
DROP. Do you wanna play? You too Zip.
ORFLONG. Yelsa.
ZIP. Silly Drop!
DROP. Come Here!

(DROP pulls ORFLONG and ZIP into a huddle at center stage.)

DROP. Zip, you start over there! Orflong you start over there! Do what I do.

(ZIP and DROP exit in the same direction. ORFLONG remains onstage still, confused.)

ZIP. *(Runs back onstage)* Onatulla! Onatulla!! [Over there! Over there!]
ORFLONG. Okaoka! [Okay!]

(ZIP and ORFLONG exit the stage.)
(DROP enters. She has a plunger on her face and she wanders around the stage as if she were a giant bird.)

DROP. Squawk! Squawk!

(ZIP enters watching DROP.)

DROP. Zip! The birds go squawk! Squawk!!
ZIP. Squawk! Squawk!!

(DROP begins to lead ZIP in a follow the leader sort of game.)

DROP. The birds go squawk! The birds go flap, flap!
ZIP. The biirds go squawk! The birds go flap, flap!

(ORFLONG enters carrying his plunger. He is confused about how to play the game.)

DROP. Orflong! The birds go flap, flap! The birds go squawk, squawk!!
ZIP. Biirds go flap! Flap! Birds go squawk! Squawk!!

(Pause)

ORFLONG. *(Placing plunger to his face)* Dilpa?

(ZIP and DROP laugh. DROP begins to lead again. She places the plunger on her head.)

DROP. Flap flap!! Squawk Squawk!!
ZIP. Flap Flap!! Squawk squawk!!
ORFLONG. Dilpa! Dilpa!! Dilpa!!
DROP. Flap Flap!! Squawk!!
ZIP. Flap Flap!! Squawk!!
ORFLONG. Dilpa! Dilpa!! Dilpa!!

ZIP. Squawk! Flap! Squawk Squawk!!

DROP. *(Laughs)* Yes! Squawk! Flap! Squawk Squawk!!

ORFLONG. *(Pushes past ZIP in an attempt to get DROP's attention.)* Dilpa Dilpa Dilpa!!

ZIP. *(Pushes back past ORFLONG)* Squawk! Flap!!

(ORFLONG pulls ZIP to the ground. There is a struggle as ZIP and ORFLONG wrestle in a fight. After a moment, ZIP begins to tickle ORFLONG. ORFLONG gives in and begins to tickle back. They are now laughing and playing. DROP is no longer watching them. She is staring at the ground.)

DROP. Ssssssshhhhhhhh!!

ZIP. Squawk!! Squawk!!

DROP. Sssshhhh!!

ORFLONG. Dilpa! Dilpa!

DROP. SSSSSSSssshhhhhhhhh!!

(DROP has carefully placed the plunger on the ground. She taps and listens.)

ZIP. Squawk! Squawk!

DROP. SShhh!! Zip!. . . . . I think I hear a Kalakazula! Orflong. . . . . .

ZIP. Drop. . . . . .Squawk?

DROP. Wait! The Kalakazula . . . let's see . . . hmmmmmmmm . . . yes . . . it's squishing it's way over this direction. . . . I can . . . yes . . .

(She follows the ground with her plunger.)

ZIP. Ooooooooooooooo?

(DROP nods at him.)
(ZIP joins DROP and takes up her somewhat poor hunting form.)
(ZIP and DROP are now both attempting to hunt a Kalakazula.)

ORFLONG. *(Wildly runs around the stage with his beak on.)* Dilpa! Dilpa! Dilpa! Dilpa!
DROP & ZIP. Ssshhhhhhhhhhh!!!!!

(Pause)

ORFLONG. Einu fluka gonta otla calpa finu, fluka ednen eblu uquanim. [If you're going to catch one, you need to hold the pole like this.]

(ORFLONG begins to present proper hunting form to both ZIP and DROP.)

ZIP. Drop, that Kalakazula is verpa here.
DROP. *(Watching ORFLONG)* Ooooo . . . . I see . . . .
ORFLONG. Fluka pirgin nandley kilpe osna, Drop. [You grip the handle like this, Drop.]
ZIP. Ssshh!! You wwill scaare them Orflong!
ORFLONG. Fluka patsun nandley kilpe osna. [You then tap the handle very carefully.]

(DROP has started to follow ORFLONG's actions.)

DROP. Okay . . . . now . . . .

ORFLONG. Fluka sitlen cuflanaw. [Listen very carefully.]

(ZIP begins to follow ORFLONG's actions.)
(ORFLONG enjoys their interest. He is proud that ZIP & DROP finally want to learn how to hunt. ORFLONG helps ZIP with his form. He then stands back and watches for a moment. ORFLONG then turns to hunt in the opposite direction.)
(ZIP and DROP begin to make fun of ORFLONG's hunting. Whenever ORFLONG turns towards them, they pretend to follow his lead.)

ORFLONG. Ssshhhhhhh!

(Hunting procedure)
(DROP and ZIP come together behind ORFLONG and whisper to each other. They maintain the appearance of hunting. ORFLONG is completely focused on a Kalakazula. DROP and ZIP sneak up behind him and place their plungers on their faces as beaks.)

ZIP & DROP. Squawk! Squawk!! Squawk! Squawk!!

(ORFLONG jumps)
(ZIP and DROP chase one another offstage.)

DROP. Squawk! Squawk!! Flap! Flap!!
ZIP. Squawk! Squawk! Flap! Flap!!

(ORFLONG watches them go, baffled.)

ORFLONG. *(Raises plunger slowly to his face.)* Dilpa . .

(Pause)
(ORFLONG slowly returns to his hunting. A worm is near. ORFLONG exits. Quirky dance music rises as the scene changes.)
(ZIP and DROP enter, playing. They play a foreign version of tag. ORFLONG enters and smiles at them. He walks over and begins clearing away a nice spot on the ground for dinner. ORFLONG walks over and directs ZIP to a specific spot on the ground. ORFLONG then walks over and directs DROP to a specific seat on the ground. ORFLONG then exits.)
(Pause. ZIP and DROP giggle, a bit confused.)
(ORFLONG re-enters, carrying several dishes of Kalakazula.)

ORFLONG. Kalakazula! *(Pause)* Kalakazula!
DROP. Hmmmmmmmmmmmmmmmmmmmm ....
ZIP. MMMMMM..my favoorite Orflong, Kalakazula.

(ZIP wiggles the Kalakazula around the stage making it come to life. DROP laughs.)

ORFLONG. *(Smiles)* Kalakazula.
DROP. These really aren't that awful once you get used to them. How did you prepare these Orflong?
ORFLONG. Fluka urla? [What's that?]
DROP. Well, whatever you did, it's wonderful.
ORFLONG. AA kinth AA aymal vahme scovna welna rea ot gid orfnu Kalakazula. Zip salap llearan kelup

Kalakazula. [I think I may have discovered a new area to dig for Kalakazula. Zip has never really liked Kalakazula.]

DROP. Oooooooo.....

ZIP. Mmmmmmmmyummmmmmmmyummmmmmmm.

(ZIP chews, Kalakazula falling from his mouth.)
(DROP laughs)

ORFLONG. Drop. . Zip, Kalakazula lapre veralka rehreh upa Kalakazula herf veralka rehreh ... Aaaaauuuuuugh! *(ORFLONG smashes the food into his mouth. ORFLONG laughs.)* [Drop ... Zip, Kalakazula over here, and Kalakazula over here and they both fly into my mouth!]

(Pause)

DROP. What did he say Zip?

ZIP. Oh, he said that...

(Pause)
(ZIP stares at ORFLONG)
(ZIP doesn't know what ORFLONG has said.)

DROP. What's that Zip?

(Pause)

ZIP. *(Stares at ORFLONG)* He said that . . . .

(Pause)

DROP. Zip?

ZIP. He said that . . . he wanted to tell you the story of how he got his name.

DROP. Really?

ORFLONG. Urla? [What?]

(Pause)

ZIP. You see, there's this fruit on our planet called Orff fruit. They are pink fruits with little itty-bitty black dots on them. Bitty-itty bitty-itty dots!

(DROP laughs as ZIP demonstrates.)

ORFLONG. Zip! Urla unasay perfa fluka? [Zip! What are you talking about?]

ZIP. *(Stares at ORFLONG) (Pause)* Anyway, Orflong and I were very very young and we were playing undreneath this Orff tree. Do you remember that Orflong?

ORFLONG. Urla? [What?]

(Pause)

ZIP. Anyway, we were playing under an Orff tree and an Orff fell from the tree and hit Orflong on the head. Now, Drop, I know you might be getting confused as I described an Orff fruit that hit Orflong under the Orff tree. *(DROP is laughing)* But, this Orff that hit Orflong was no ordinary Orff. It was huge! And it hit Orflong and I picked up the fruit and shouted ORFLONG! And then Orflong shouted ORFLONG! And then Orflong became Orflong's name!

(DROP laughs)

ORFLONG. Zip, walunup reap fluka alkanu bulpe? [Zip, what are you talking about?]

(Pause)

ZIP. *(Stares at ORFLONG.)* Orflong! Orflong! Orflong! *(ZIP begins to yell this in an attempt to remember his own language)* Orflong! Orflong! Orflong! Orflong! Orflong! Orflong! Orflong! Orflong! Orflong!

(DROP laughs. She joins ZIP, thinking that he is playing a game. ZIP continues to scream the name.)

ZIP & DROP. ORFLONG! ORFLONG! ORFLONG! ORFLONG! ORFLONG! ORFLONG! ORFLONG! ORFLONG! ORFLONG!

(Pause)
(ZIP stares at ORFLONG)

DROP. Zip, are you done with your Kalakazula? *(Pause)* Zip? Are you finished with your Kalakazula?

ZIP. Yep. . . Now how about some Orflong. *(He runs over and begins munching on ORFLONG's head.)* Mmmmmmm .... big Orff!

ORFLONG. *(Confused)* Tulna bulka rufa dolkon? [What's going on.]

DROP. *(Rising)* Hey Zip, do you wanna dance?

(DROP begins to dance. Music rises, very low.)
(ZIP stops and stares at ORFLONG)
(Pause)

ORFLONG. Zip, umun einba.... [Zip, my friend....]

(ORFLONG places his hand on his heart and then on ZIP's)
(Pause. ZIP and ORFLONG stare at one another.)
(ZIP looks at DROP.)
(Pause)
(ZIP goes to DROP. She signals for music. It is the same music that ORFLONG and ZIP danced to in the beginning. ZIP and DROP dance.)
(ORFLONG sits and watches. ZIP and DROP dance to the quirky music. They dance around where ORFLONG is sitting. ORFLONG slowly rises. Pause. ORFLONG watches ZIP and DROP. He begins to slowly exit. He looks at ZIP and DROP one last time and slowly exits. A moment after ORFLONG exits there is a dark blue flash of light. ORFLONG is gone. ZIP and DROP stop dancing. ZIP stares at where ORFLONG exited. ZIP looks around the planet. He then looks at DROP. The music is gone. DROP stares at ZIP. ZIP looks back to where ORFLONG exited at. The lights slowly fade to black.)

The End

PRODUCTION SUGGESTIONS

The following notes are suggestions. Included are design and directorial concepts that worked. Anyone choosing to produce DROP is welcome to consider these possibilities. These are only suggestions.

SCENIC DESIGN – visually, the play is strongest with a very sparse setting. In the Kennedy Center production of DROP, three styrofoam rocks, large enough to stand on, were used. These helped to give the director some levels to work with as well as some sense of the world of the play.

LIGHTING DESIGN – the lighting in the Kennedy Center production was hugely beneficial in creating the Gavanuuyian world. A large Cyclorama was hung and lit in a different color for each scene.

PROPERTIES – With the central prop, the plungers, a little paint can go a long way in making the tool/toy truly Gavanuuyian. A loaf of French Bread sliced just right can create marverous Kalakazula worms for the final scene of the play.

MUSIC – The choice of music is crucial as it takes us in and out of scenes. Music in the original production was both original and found. A great place to look is among catalogues of space and and surf-rock.

COSTUME PLOT

ORFLONG:
Entire play; black, full-body leotard. A black skull-cap made from the same material. Navy-blue sneakers that blend with costume.

ZIP:
Entire play; black, full-body leotard. A black skull-cap made from the same material. Navy-blue sneakers that blend with costume.

DROP:
Entire play; sleeveless, black, body leotard. Lined with several colored pieces of cotton cloth to form a sort of skirt. Dark shoes.

PROPERTIES PLOT

Scene One – Hunting Kalakazula
ORFLONG: Plunger (Note: The plungers are regular toilet plungers attached to a larger handle of either a broom or a mop.)
ZIP: Two plungers

Scene Two – Paintings
ORFLONG: Leaf journal
ZIP: Leaf journal and eight or more leaf paintings

Scene Three – Pillish
    ZIP: Two plungers and one long piece of rope

Scene Four – Picnic
    ORFLONG & DROP: One picnic cloth, crackers & jelly

Scene Five – Drop Hunts
    DROP: Plunger
    ZIP: Two plungers and rope

Scene Six – Jump rope
    DROP: Rope

Scene Seven – Sleep
    ORFLONG: Leaf journal
    ZIP: Leaf journal
    DROP: Sleep blanket

Scene Eight – Gerfle
    ZIP: Plunger
    ORFLONG: Plunger and Game-ball

Scene Nine – Drop's Bird-game
    DROP, ORFLONG & ZIP: Plunger

Scene Ten – Kalakazula Dinner
    DROP, ZIP & ORFLONG:
        Leaf plate with loaf of French bread cut to look
        like a Kalakazula worm.

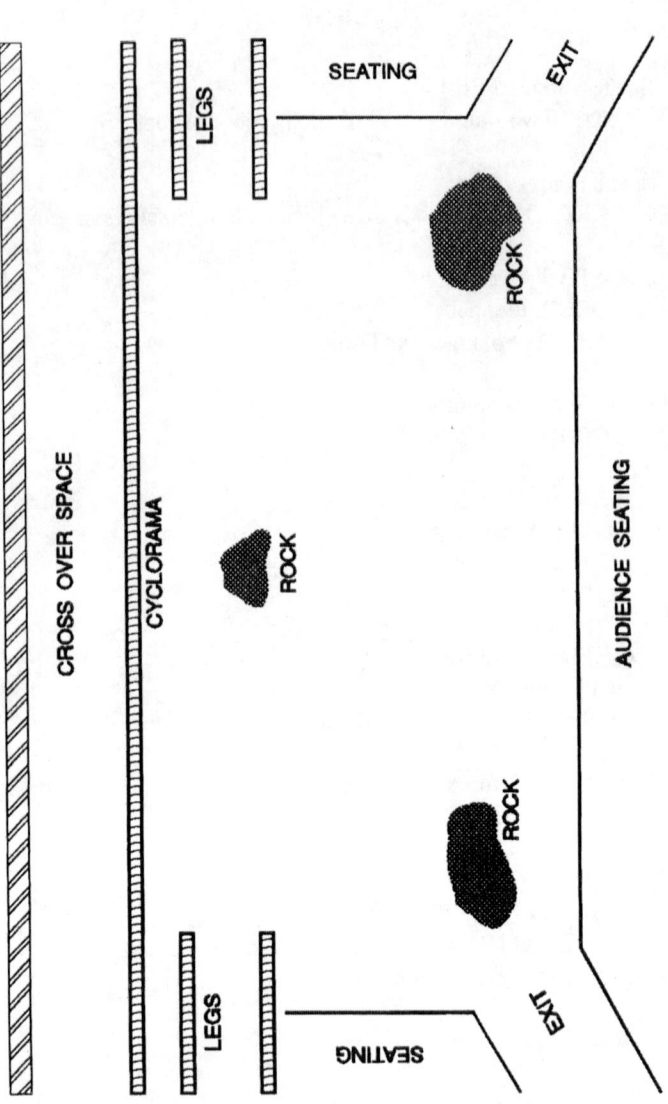

Basic Ground Plan for 3/4 Seating or Proscenium